DISCOVERING
FROGS

DOUGLAS FLORIAN

CHARLES SCRIBNER'S SONS
NEW YORK

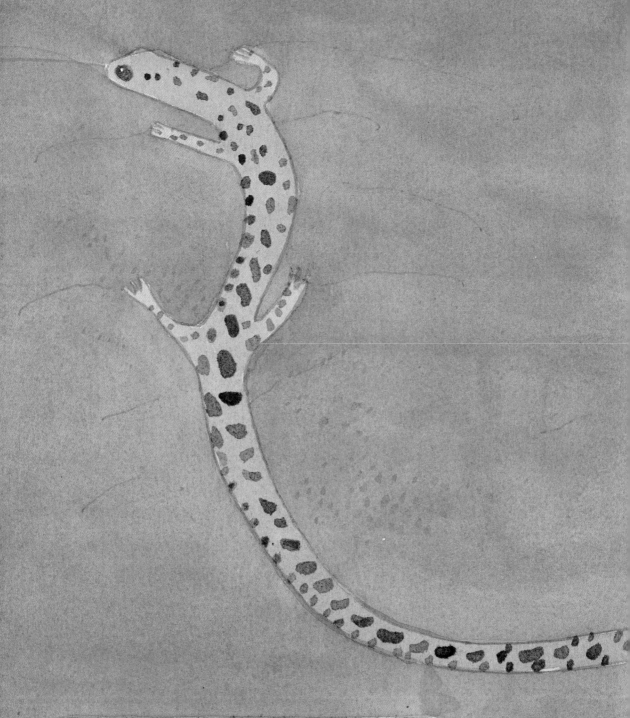

This picture is 2 times life-size

Millions of years ago a group of animals called *amphibians* (am-fi-bee-ans) were the first to rise out of the water and live both on land and in water. Even today, amphibians are born in water. Only as adults can they survive on land.

The salamander, the frog, and the kind of frog called a toad are all amphibians. In order to stay alive they have to keep their skins moist, so most of them live near water.

Salamanders have thin bodies and long tails. The Long-tailed Salamander lives in damp caves and near streams.

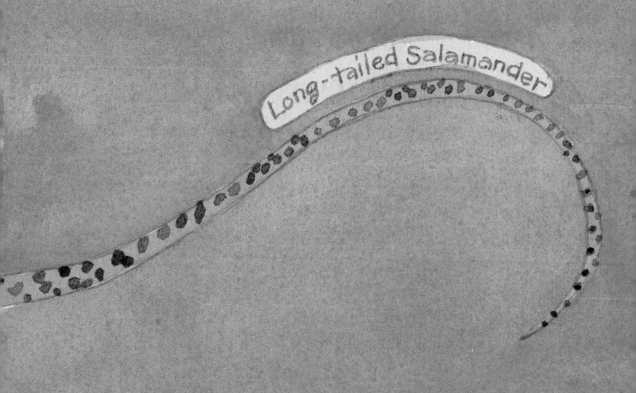

Long-tailed Salamander

Gray Treefrog

Adult frogs and toads don't have tails, and their legs are stronger than a salamander's. Frogs are usually thinner than toads, and their skin is usually smoother. Frogs have longer legs than toads. This helps them jump farther. The Gray Treefrog jumps from branch to branch.

The Southwestern Toad moves in short hops.

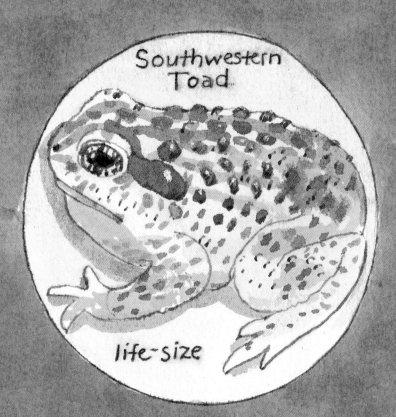

Southwestern Toad

life-size

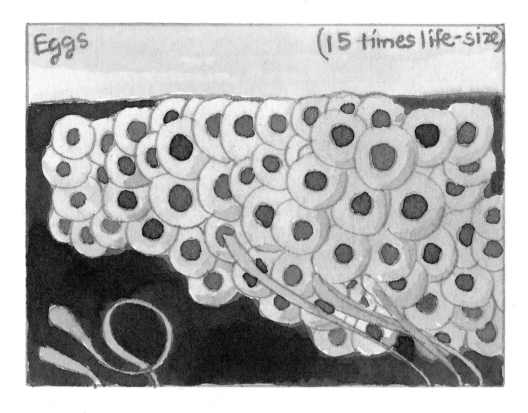

Most frogs begin their lives inside eggs under water. Several eggs are held together by a clear jelly that protects them. Sometimes the eggs are attached to underwater plants.

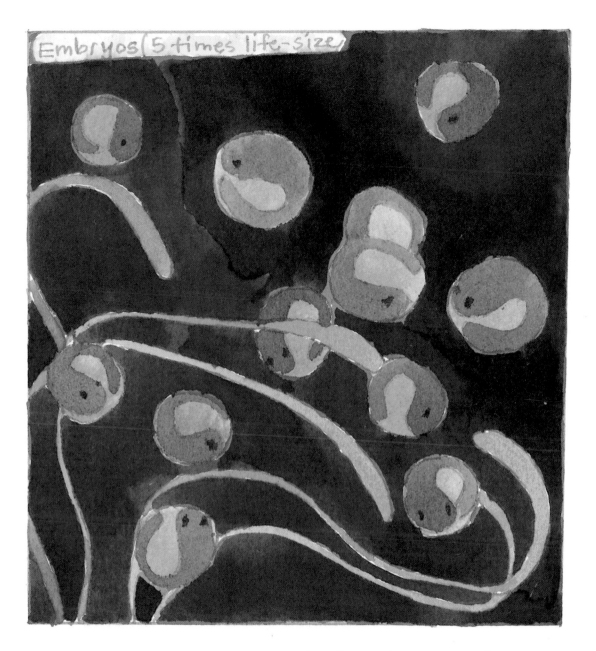

Inside the egg an *embryo* (em-bree-o) is growing. One end becomes a head while the other grows into a tail.

After about two or three weeks the embryo hatches from the egg. Now it is called a *tadpole*.

The tadpole breathes oxygen from the water, and it has a long tail to help it swim.

The tadpole continues to grow. With its small mouth it eats tiny plants that live in the water.

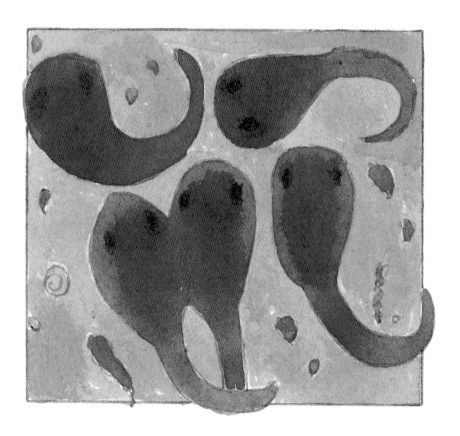

After about six weeks two back legs start to grow. The tadpole's mouth and eyes are larger. Soon two front legs grow. The tadpole is getting ready to live on land.

When the tadpole finally comes out of the water, it is a baby frog. Now it has a nose and lungs to breathe the air. Its tail will get smaller and smaller until it disappears.

Once a frog is an adult, it can mate. The female lays her eggs in the water. The male's sperm joins with the eggs to *fertilize* them. Only a fertile egg can grow into a frog.

Most frogs do very little to protect their eggs. One exception is the Midwife Toad, found in Europe. After the male toad has fertilized the female's eggs, it attaches them to his back legs. About a month later, it takes the eggs to a pond, where they hatch. Then he swims away, his work done.

The moist skin of frogs is very important, because oxygen is taken from the air through the skin.

There is a wide variety in the color of frogs. Usually a frog's color is like the color of the plants or ground where it lives. This Southern Cricket Frog looks a lot like the plants it sits on.

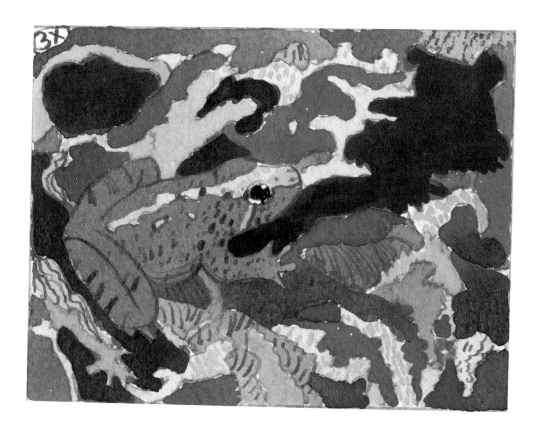

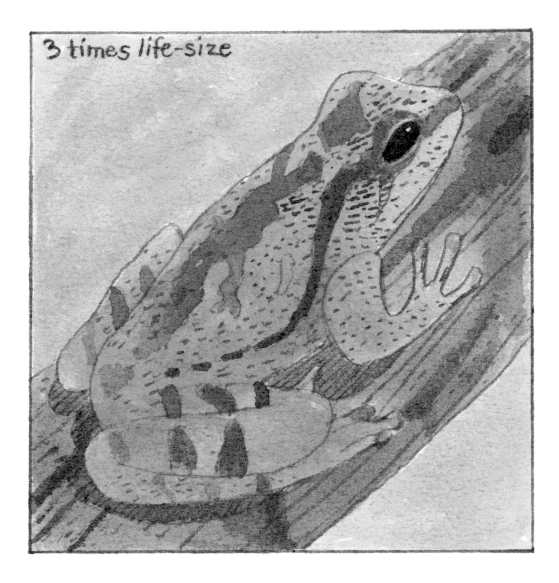

3 times life-size

This Pine-woods Treefrog is hard to see when it sits still on this branch. This gives the frog protection or *camouflage* (cam-o-flodge).

3 times life-size

The eyes of a frog bulge out of its head. This helps it to see in different directions without moving its head. Sometimes a frog sits under the water with only its eyes and nose above the surface.

3 times life-size

Behind their eyes frogs have ears. The two flat circles are the eardrums of the frog. The Green Frog's ears are quite large. In other frogs the ears may be difficult to see.

Male frogs have one or two pouches of skin called vocal sacs. These fill up with air to help make the voice of the frog sound louder. Male frogs croak to attract a female mate. A Spring Peeper's voice sounds like a high whistle. It can be heard from a mile away.

Spring Peeper
2 times life-size

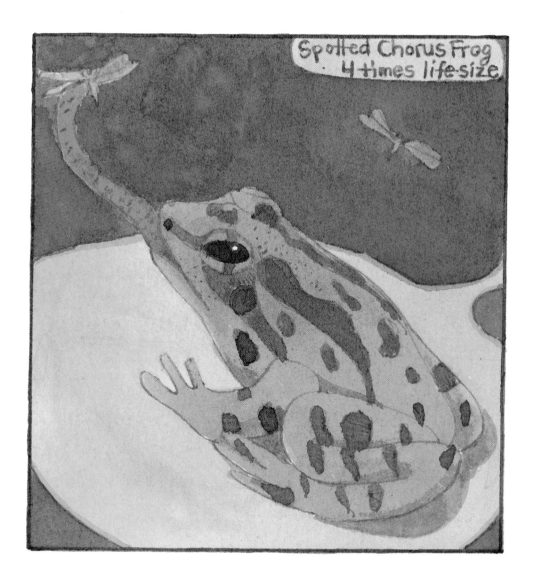

To catch an insect a frog uses its long sticky tongue. The tongue rolls out, sticks onto the insect, and rolls back into the frog's mouth. All this happens in less than one second.

Frogs are very good at jumping. This helps them escape from animals quickly. The long back legs of a frog act like springs.

Leopard Frog

The Southern Cricket Frog is less than one inch long, but it can jump three feet. The Leopard Frog of North America jumps more than five feet.

CARPENTER FROG

2 times life-size

To help them swim, many frogs have webbed back feet. Webbed feet have flaps of skin between the toes. The flaps push against the water when the frog is swimming.

Some frogs have a poison in their skin. One is the Arrow-poison Frog of South America. An animal may die if it tries to eat this frog. Its bright colors are a signal to animals that it is poisonous to eat.

5 times life-size

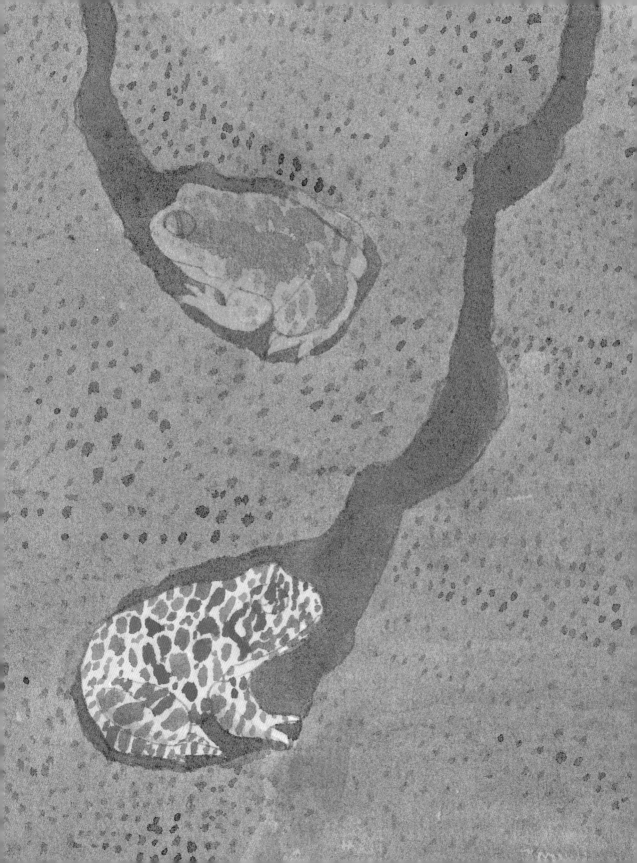

Frogs, like other amphibians, are *cold-blooded*. This means that the temperature inside their bodies changes when the temperature outside changes.

When the weather gets cold, frogs dig burrows under the ground or in the mud at the bottom of ponds. Here they sleep, breathing very slowly, living off the fat stored in their bodies. This is called *hibernation*. In spring, the frog goes back to its active life.

There are sixteen *families* of frogs. One family is called the Narrow-mouthed Frogs. They usually spend the daytime underground and come out at night to eat and breed. Their pointed noses help them dig up ants to eat.

The Burrowing Frog of South Africa is in this family. When this frog is frightened, it puffs itself up with air to make itself look bigger.

4 times lifesize

The Great Plains Narrow-mouthed Frog is found in the Southwest and in Mexico. It sometimes shares a cool burrow with a mole or a lizard.

Treefrogs are a family of frogs that can live in trees. Their thin bodies help them keep balanced on branches. They have big round *toe pads* that help them stick to almost anything. Living up in trees keeps these frogs protected from many animals that might attack them.

The Pacific Treefrog can change its colors to blend into different places. It lives in the states west of the Rocky Mountains.

2 times life-size

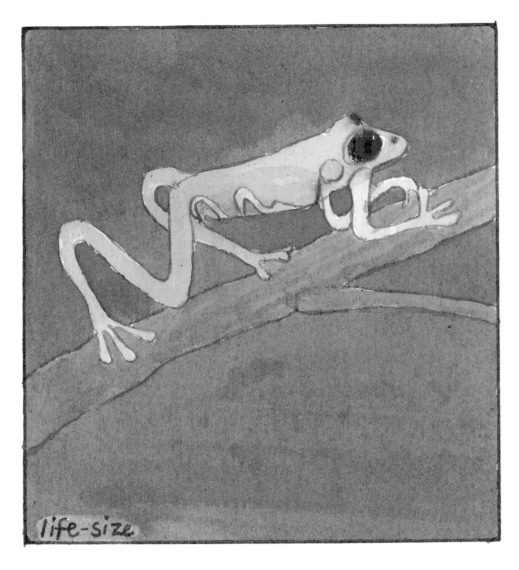

life-size

The Red-eyed Treefrog of Central America has very thin long legs. These are good for walking along branches but not for jumping.

Little Grass Frog
(life-size)

The smallest frog of North America is the Little Grass
Frog. It is only about half an inch long. It usually stays close
to the ground, although it is in the Treefrog family.

The largest North American frog is the Bullfrog. It grows up to eight inches long. The large circles behind a Bullfrog's eyes are its ears. Bullfrogs have been known to eat small birds, baby turtles, and even other frogs. You can find them in ponds and lakes.

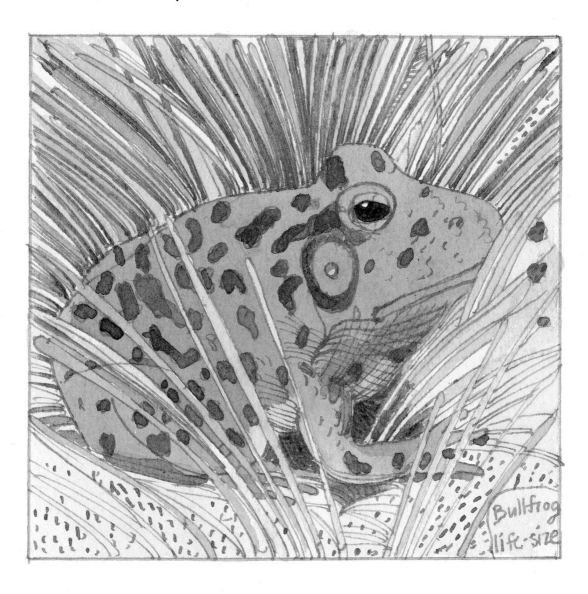

Today there are 2,700 different kinds of frogs in the world, but the lives of many are in danger. Water pollution is harmful to frogs, because chemicals in the water can easily get through their thin skin into their bodies. Each year many ponds and lakes, the places where they live, are filled in with land by people making buildings and highways. If we want frogs to survive, we have to protect the places where they live.

For Louise and Sammy

Charles Scribner's Sons Books for Young Readers
Macmillan Publishing Company
866 Third Avenue, New York, NY 10022
Collier Macmillan Canada, Inc.

Printed in Japan by Toppan Printing Co.
First Edition

10 9 8 7 6 5 4 3 2 1

Library of Congress Cataloging-in-Publication Data
Florian, Douglas.   Discovering frogs.
Summary: Discusses the development and behavior of frogs and introduces several varieties.
1. Frogs—Juvenile literature. [1. Frogs] I. Title.
QL668.E2F48 1986   597.8   86-6731
ISBN 0-684-18688-8